Lord, Help Me With My Negative Emotions:
A Guide To Controlling Your Emotions And Finding Peace In The Midst of Storms
(Deliver Me Series Book 2)

Lynn R. Davis

PUBLISHED BY: Lynn R Davis

Be the first to know when my books are free. Visit: LynnRDavis.com today to register your email address.

Contents

Introduction

Emotional bondage is the worst type slavery. Every negative circumstance becomes your master. Whenever something or someone triggers your negative reaction, you become like a puppet on a string. Your feelings easily manipulate you into behaving in a way that only hurts you and the people around you. It's time for a change.

Is this book for you? Here's how you can tell. You, or someone you know, responds to negative people or circumstances by:

**Sobbing until your head hurts
**Going off
**Losing it
**Throwing a fit
** Breaking things
**Yelling
**Hitting
**Seeking revenge at all cost
**Slashing tires
**Pulling out a pistol
**Becoming depressed
**Losing sleep

If any of those sound like you, then you should take steps today to change how you handle your negative emotions. There is an alternative positive response for every negative emotion you face. I know many will disagree with this particular work because we have accepted that our environment, people, and circumstances control our emotions. And because of that, our emotional responses can only improve when our environment improves. I disagree.

Based on personal experience, I believe it's possible to respond positively in the most negative of situations. Having experienced the big D's in my life: Death, Divorce, and Depression, I fully understand emotional pain. In every instance, I felt like crawling under a rock and never coming out again. But I came out from under the rock. I smiled again. I loved again. I lived life again.

Take Paul and Silas, when they were locked in prison. They chose to sing and pray rather than lament and lose emotional control. There are many other Biblical examples and we will look at some of them in this book. Like these great examples, I believe we too can keep our cool and not fall apart every time our environment falls apart.

I'm not saying that I never sought professional help. Before I got my emotions under control, I took anti-depressants for a short time. Some people will need professional help and they should not feel ashamed about seeking it. What I am saying is, the "help" I received wasn't what delivered me. I believe my ability to overcome was the result of faith. It was God's love that brought me out of the darkness of depression and back into the light of His love and acceptance.

This book is for people who have tried and failed at controlling emotions but aren't ready to give up.

Use this scripture as a mantra:

Psalm 34:19 says, "*MANY ARE THE AFFLICTIONS of the righteous, but the LORD delivers him out of them all.*"
Plug in the word **emotional** right before **afflictions** and read it again:
Many are the [emotional] afflictions of the righteous, but the LORD delivers him out of them all.

Now, ask God to help you believe that you are emotionally healed.

Chapter 1: Control Your Emotions or They Will Control You

"What worries you, masters you."- unknown

The Power Of Your Emotions

When emotions are uncontrolled, they wreak havoc. It only takes seconds for an outburst of negative emotion to tear a relationship to shreds. If allowed, damaging emotions like jealousy, anger, or insecurity will take control and burn like wild fire.

I remember, years ago, when I found out that a boyfriend was cheating. My emotions ranged from sadness and depression to jealousy and rage. I thought about throwing all his clothes into the courtyard of our complex. Then, I contemplated calling all of his family and friends and telling them what a lying, cheating jerk I saw him as. I was ticked off and I was ready to play judge and jury. Never mind the role I played in the demise of the relationship.

I was confused. I wondered what I had done wrong. My emotions were all over the place. Now, years later, when I think about it, I'm amazed that I came out of that situation in one piece. It was hard. It hurt like heck, but I'm here to tell you about it. I survived and so can you.

One of the keys to controlling emotions is knowing that you don't have to be at the mercy of your circumstance or situation. The natural tendency is to overreact or respond in ways that do more harm than good. Sure, in the short term, you feel vindicated, but if you truly are a man or woman of God, you can never be at peace with acting out of retaliation or vengeance.

Uncontrolled negative emotions can often lead to heated arguments, or worse. We've all seen the horrible true stories on crime TV of people whose emotions got the best of them. And then later, in the interviews, they wish they'd just walked away or made some other decision.

Think of a time when you were in a bad situation. Or maybe you're in one now. Did you have trouble controlling your emotions then? Are you having trouble right now controlling your emotions, even though you know you should?

God doesn't want you to suffer. He doesn't want you to hurt yourself or anyone else. He knows you are hurting. He knows you want to feel vindicated. But He doesn't want you to make the situation worse. He doesn't want to see you suffer more than you are in this moment. So He's encouraging you to take control. Try to detach yourself from the negative emotion and re-attach yourself to His word.

*Many are the [**emotional**] afflictions of the righteous, but the LORD delivers him out of them all.*

Do something to take your mind off the situation. Read your Bible. Watch your favorite televangelist. Listen to music. Go for a walk to clear your head. And if you need to cry, cry. If you just have to talk to someone, call a trusted mentor or person you *really* trust.

Someone who will help you keep a level head. The last person you need to contact is an emotionally charged acquaintance who slashes tires and keys cars. You can come out on top, even if you cry buckets of tears and feel like your heart is shattered. God heals and His Son comforts us. "In the world you have tribulation, but take courage; I HAVE OVERCOME THE WORLD." (John 16:33)

With everything I was faced with, shame, embarrassment, fear of loneliness, betrayal, etc., I still worked hard to control the negative emotions that bombarded me constantly. I didn't go all Angela Basset from *Waiting to Exhale* or Sandra Bullock from *Hope Floats*.

Yes, I yelled at him. And I most certainly told him a thing or two about himself. I was hurt and, quite honestly, I wanted him to suffer.
I didn't think I would ever be able to forgive him or the other woman. But I kept my composure. I remembered God's word, "THE LORD IS NEAR TO THE BROKENHEARTED AND SAVES THE CRUSHED IN SPIRIT." (PSALM 34:18) I asked God to handle it and I trusted Him to keep his promise. It took months and months for me to get over the pain. But I did. I began to notice that it didn't hurt as much. And, one day, I woke up with the memory but the pain was gone. Today, he and I can laugh and talk without rehearsing the past. The Lord really does heal broken hearts.
Emotions Can Help You And Hinder You. To be successful and competent, in personal and professional relationships, you have to be able to control emotions. More often than not, you will be judged based on your ability to deal with emotions, especially in difficult times. People who are able to keep their emotions in check, even when the chips are down, advance further in life, personally, professionally, and spiritually.

Emotions aren't all bad. Anger and fear are very strong emotions. In scripture, we repeatedly see "fear not". But in regard to anger, we are told, "Be angry but sin not." I think that's because fear is more of a debilitating emotion. It opens the door for doubt. And our faith doesn't work when we doubt. Fear tends to stop me in my tracks whereas anger, when controlled, motivates me to change or improve. When my marriage ended, I was angry that I had to start over, move in with my dad, and pay a pile of debts. But I directed that anger toward improving my situation. I applied to graduate school, created a debt management plan, and eventually was able to purchase a home.

My trust in God kept the fear at bay. My faith helped me control and redirect my anger toward solving my problems rather than creating more. We really do have to make the choice to control our emotions. No matter how stressed or pressured we become, we can't let our environment threaten our emotional stability or how we react under pressure.

I had a manager once who was super good at what he did. We worked in a small group but were responsible for managing project resources for hundreds of employees that equated to millions of dollars. The job was stressful at times. Although our manager was good at budgeting and resource management, he had a tendency to fly off the handle when things went wrong. Whenever there was a problem with the reports or numbers, we knew that someone would be yelled at. We'd witnessed more than one employee leaving his office in tears.

This went on for almost a year before I finally found a position elsewhere. Not long after, I ran into one of my ex-team members in the cafeteria. She was grinning from ear to ear. Apparently that manager had been fired because of a formal complaint that was filed about his uncontrolled temper. The company saw him as a liability. She went on to say that he'd been fired from other jobs and passed over for promotions because of his temper. Instead of controlling his emotions, he was allowing them to control him. And they were hindering his career.

Our lives are so fast paced and we come across so many different situations in any given day. When we start out, we may have a clear mind and know what we have to achieve to be productive on that day. However, life unfolds before us and before we know it our plans change. In an instant, we are faced with a situation that irritates us, disappoints us, frustrates us, or annoys us. At these moments, it's important to be in control of how we respond. Always remember that no one else is controlling this for you. You might feel that they are "pushing your buttons", but you are ultimately responsible for what happens next.

Emotions are temporary states of mind, don't let them permanently destroy you.

Our emotions have triggers. Meaning, something ignites them. Emotions will take you over if you allow them to, yet, these emotions only strike when triggered. Every day, someone struggles with emotions. Many people find it difficult to manage these emotions.

Strength doesn't come from what you can do. It comes from overcoming the things you once thought you couldn't.

Some people have medical or mental related complications that pose challenges for them when it comes to controlling emotions. Let me encourage you. If you think you have a medical condition, talk to a healthcare professional. There are many options out there. God created doctors but as I always say, physicians don't have the final word in your healing-God does. But if you feel overwhelmed and think there may be some other issue going on besides stress, talk to someone and at least eliminate the possibility of a medical condition that may require treatment.

Realize that some of the best tools to control your emotions resides inside of you. You can master your emotions by exploring positive self-talk, scripture meditation, prayer, etc. Make it a choice to master the emotional reactions that cause anger, fear, resentment, doubt, and so on. Find ways to limit your exposure to negative triggers and people.

What's On Your Mind?

Our thoughts are the source. That's why 2 Corinthians 10:5 warns us to cast down every thought and imagination that is contrary to the word. Evil thoughts, when pondered, conceive negative emotions and those negative emotions birth unhealthy reactions. But if we heed 2 Corinthians 10:5 and cast that negative thought down and replace it with the word of God, positive emotions are conceived and healthy emotional responses are born instead.

Sometimes, we respond the way society has told us we should respond when we go through a tough time. Society says its okay to be "pissed off" when someone cuts you off in traffic or takes your parking space. It's "acceptable" understandable to verbally abuse others if that's what you experienced growing it. Depression is after the death of a loved one is expected. No one blames us if we become bitter after a bad break up or divorce. You get the point. Society says our situation dictate our emotions. But the word of God says we should be in control of our emotions. Our feelings can't be allowed to control us. **"A fool loses his temper, but a wise man holds it back." Proverbs 29:11**

So if you have these thoughts and ideas that you're supposed to react negatively when certain things happen, then you're going to do just that-react negatively. Take guilt for instance. It's an emotion based in fear. Fear that you've done something so wrong that you cannot be forgiven. That idea goes against the word of God. It's good that you feel something about the wrong that you've done. Let the guilty feeling be a signal that something is or was wrong and should be address. Then you address it. Confess it. And move on.

"There is therefore no condemnation to them who are in Christ Jesus."
(Romans 8:1)

Emotions Don't Have To Dictate Our Actions

Emotions, like the tongue, can bless us or destroy us. Proverbs 18:21 says life and death are in the power of the tongue. The words we speak can give life or cause death. So it's imperative that we choose our words carefully. But, some times more than others, it can be difficult to control our tongues because of our emotions. Proverbs 29:11 says, "A fool gives full vent to his spirit, but a wise man quietly holds it back." This leads me to believe that God considers us wise when we are able to control our emotions. And by doing so, it will be that much easier to control the words that leave our lips.

We can't let our emotions rule us. Emotions can be controlled. We don't have to let them dictate how we respond to the issues in our life. Just because someone breaks your heart doesn't mean you allow negative emotions of depression, defeat, or bitterness overwhelm you. Don't crawl into a ball and let life pass you by. Be thankful that you Mr. or Ms. Wrong are no longer taking up space in your life. You deserve better. And now that they have vacated, you have room in your life for the perfect mate.

God doesn't want us to just go with the flow of whatever emotion we are feeling at any given time. Can you imagine what the world would be like if we all just acted on our emotions? I know there are some schools of thought that tell us to just feel the emotion.

But personally, I've noticed that when I allow myself to "feel" the emotion, I am bombarded with even more negative emotion. And the more I focus on the negative feelings, the worse I feel. There's just nothing good about getting all worked up and upset whenever something doesn't go my way. So I decided a long time ago that I was going to do the opposite of what I felt. Instead of crying my eyes out I was going to laugh. If I wanted to yell, I prayed and spoke calmly instead. Life has been a lot better. I encourage you to try it. When your emotions flair, instead of reacting the way you normally would, do the opposite. Of course your kids may think you've been alien abducted, but hey that's okay. They will come to love and appreciate the new and improved emotionally healthy you.

An example of doing the opposite is what Jesus told us to do in the midst of turmoil, he said, "Be of good cheer," Christ wasn't saying, "Pretend that everything is great." He was telling us things may look bad right now but be joyful because you already have the victory! Then in John 14:1, He encouraged the disciples, "Let not our hearts be troubled." I don't know about you, but I watched the movie, *The Passion of The Christ*, and that made me cry. How in the world could the disciples see it first hand and not be troubled? Yet, that is what Jesus told them. That was His expectation for the. That they not be troubled even though they were having an emotionally gut-wrenching experience. I believe today Jesus is still telling us not to let ourselves become overwhelmed by negative emotions- not to be troubled. And if he's telling us not to allow it, then we must have the power within us to overcome troubled emotions.

We have to stop justifying falling apart.

The way we respond at the beginning of a crisis determines whether or not we win the battle with that circumstance. It's critical that we don't fall apart. Hindsight is 20/20. We often see our emotional breakdown was clearly a mistake after the damage is already done.

Take control at the beginning with the understanding that you have choices when it comes to emotions. That negative emotion that you are feeling is *not* the only emotion you have to feel. When you feel your emotions overtaking you, stop and say, "God told me to rejoice always."

Say this, *"David blessed the Lord at all times and praised God continually. I will bless and praise God at all times. Even when my emotions are tempting me to be negative, I will rejoice!"*

When we go through a challenge in life, we experience a range of thoughts, emotions, and physical effects. The key to successfully dealing with the circumstance is learning to control those thoughts and emotions. Easier said than done? Yes, until you reach the point where your default response is the word of God. As soon as you are hit with a negative emotion, instead of giving in to it, you automatically ask yourself, ***"What does God want me to do in this situation?*** He certainly wouldn't slash a boyfriend's tires; hack into a girlfriends email; or punch a rude neighbor's lights out.

Your Emotions aren't wrong or sinful, they're human nature. People can be irritating. And our human nature, the fleshly man is weak. And quite honestly sometimes, we don't feel like doing the right thing. But that's the mediocrity of the flesh. It wants immediate gratification. It wants revenge. And it wants to see somebody suffer-now. The problem is that immediate negative emotional gratification takes a toll on our hearts. It blocks our blessings. And threatens our relationship with the Father. Lay aside every weight and sin that so easily besets you. Panic, fear, grief, sadness, anger, they all threaten to "easily beset you". Don't let them. If you're living a life of uncontrolled emotions, you're living a mediocre life. And nowhere in scripture does God tell us to live a mediocre existence.

Whether you've just been fired or experienced a bad break up, instead of replaying the every detail of what went wrong, try something different. Make a different choice. Instead of focusing on the bad, find the good. Realize that God has promised to make everything work together for your good. And that He tells us to be of good cheer because He has overcome the world. When you do this, you're casting down negative thoughts and controlling negative emotions. You are not allowing depression, anger, or resentment to set in. You're in control.

Galatians 5:16 -Walk in the spirit and you shall not walk in the flesh. Lust in the Bible isn't always sexual. Lust is a strong overpowering desire. You can have a strong overpowering desire to slap a rude waitress. But that doesn't mean you should. Just because the negative emotion exists doesn't mean it has to be acted upon. Don't indulge lustful thoughts either. Even if you are saying, "I'll never really slap anyone." It's very dangerous to meditate on negativity. You open the door for more negative emotions to enter your mind and heart thereby increasing your chances of doing what you're thinking. Or if you're in a situation where you're sad or upset, mediating on those emotions could lead you to becoming clinically depressed or acting out in a harmful way toward yourself or others.

You're going to have to change how you think about your situation before you can control how you respond to it. Your thoughts control emotions. Actions produce experience and create an environment. As a man thinks, so is he. The Lord will keep him in perfect peace whose mind is stayed on him. Proverbs 23:7 and Isaiah 26:3

You may think that your environment is the driving force behind your negative emotions. But the Lord tells us again and again in scripture to rejoice in tribulation. If we are instructed to rejoice in tribulation, then we must have a choice, right? When posed with a problem, we can decide to fall apart or fall on our knees. We can react negatively or respond positively. Let's end the chapter with a couple of examples:

Negative Emotion Reaction:
I'm all alone. I will never fall in love again. No one loves me. I don't want to live anymore.

Positive Emotional Response:
I will not let my heart be troubled. I believe in the love of God. His love is filling every void in my heart. I believe also in the resurrecting power of Jesus Christ. I am fearfully wonderfully made and I know that God can resurrect a healthy relationship in my life. I rejoice in the Lord always. God is going to work this situation out for my good.

Negative Emotion Reaction:
I don't have job. How am I going to feed my family? I'm going to lose my home. My identity is gone.

Positive Emotional Response:
Promotion comes from God. (Psalm 75:6-7) He is my source and my Jehovah Jireh. He will provide. I am God's masterpiece (Ephesians 2:10). My identity is in Christ Jesus and I am more than a conqueror. Christ has already overcome this struggle for me. And I will be of good cheer. A better opportunity is on the way. I press on toward the goal for the prize of the upward call of God in Christ Jesus. (Philippians 3:14)

Chapter 2: Second Hand Stress Kills

Some people don't necessarily mean you any harm, but they don't do you any good either. It's called dead weight. Remove it.

Dealing With Other People's Stress

If I had to say anything about the subject of other people's stress, it would be this: it's not your responsibility. I know, we are our brother's keeper and many will disagree, but we are to be supportive and offer Godly council, not pick up the burden and carry it as if it were our own. We should give our stress and burdens to the Lord, not each other. The effects of stress can be emotional. And it's hard enough for us to manage our own stress but when you have someone in your life who can't handle theirs, and they continually lean on you (or to put it more honestly - mire you down in their stressed-out world), it can be equally harmful and toxic. I'm talking beyond the occasional "shoulder to cry on". I mean, for instance, if you see them coming and you pray, *"Dear God, I really don't want to hear about xyz today!"* you're probably experiencing second hand stress.

If you are super empathetic like me, you may find yourself lying awake at night thinking about someone else's problems. The best thing to do pray for them. Offer support and resources if you are blessed to do so. But don't take on so much that you become an emotional wreck. There are boundaries, well, there should be, when it comes to helping others. Boundaries are healthy.

Second-hand stress can affect you the same way your own stress does. I remember I was okay when I talked to my friend about her problems the first few times because, in small doses, it's very manageable. But when I was constantly exposed to her stressed out conversation, it became overwhelming. I started feeling tired after we talked. You see stress takes a toll on your physical body and your mental state. You might even be able to recognize the stress the moment you are around a certain person because your body reacts to their presence. Maybe your shoulder tenses or your head aches. Its because your body has become conditioned to respond to them.

Depression and anxiety might be the first thing you feel when you get around this person. Their tale is always one of chaos and frustration, never peace and calm. It can make you nervous talking to them.

When you're not in their presence you may find that you feel angry more often. This is especially true if the situation they've been sharing with you is something that causes you to become angry, too. They're drama has slowly seeped into your emotions and now their crisis has suddenly become your crisis.

Physically, your body will be slammed every time you come in contact with this person. Your blood pressure may even rise when you're in a conversation with this person. This may be normal depending on the topic of conversation, but if you already suffer from blood pressure issues, it can be disastrous for you to try juggling that person's stress load plus your own challenges. You're praying and trying to stay in faith about your issues. But they aren't. And you find yourself losing faith about your own circumstances because you're being infected by their negative emotions. *"Do not be deceived: Bad company ruins good morals. (1 Corinthians 15:33)*

Did you know that diabetes and heart disease are often associated with stress levels? And if you already have challenges with either one of these conditions, then being around stressed out people can be harmful to your health. Your prayers for healing are being compromised by the negativity that is infiltrating your soul. Everyone experiences stress but when you surround yourself with high-stressed emotionally-uncontrolled individuals, you're overdosing and it won't be healthy for you.

I recently heard another term "contagious stress". I think that's another good way to describe when others can project or pass their negative stress on to you. Contagious stress isn't stemming from your own life, but from someone else's. Because the stressed out person is in your life, you catch it easily, and many times, you become just as stressed.

A co-worker was having marital problems. Every day, she came to work stressed. She could hardly discuss her situation without beginning to cry. At first, I was very attentive and supportive. But somewhere between the third and fourth week of being around her, I began to feel drained. After work, I was exhausted and could hardly help my son with his homework. I noticed that I was becoming angry about things that hadn't bothered me before, like the neighbor's dog barking or my son forgetting to take out the garbage.

Some people don't know any better. And really need your prayers. But other folks purposely, like leeches, drain the life from you. Not only do they come to you to soothe their frustrations, but they also use you and feed off of you to get them through their tough times. Unfortunately, by doing this, they can drain you of your own good mood and faithful attitude. As a result, when something stressful happens to you in your own life, you may have trouble handling your emotions well because you're depleted of any positivity, thanks to their visit. Not only will their foul moods sway you to becoming more negative about life in general, but your new disposition also has a domino effect. You'll spread negativity to your spouse, your kids, your family, co-workers, and others. Now not only have you been contaminated, you're spreading the disease of negativity.

Types Of Second Hand Stress Relationships

Of course, we can't just ignore every stressing person in our lives. Some of those contagious people are part of our family and there's not getting rid of some of them. As the saying goes, "Families are like fudge — mostly sweet with a few nuts". As guardians, parents, and caregivers, our children's stress is our responsibility. If the young person in your life is enduring a lot of stress, with friends, schoolwork, sports, etc., then you need to shoulder the burden and help them get through the situation. But even then, there is an opportunity to teach them how to positively handle their emotions. By keeping cool and staying calm, we show them that there is a better way to handle stressful moments.

Married couples know the pressures of financial stress can cause emotions to flare. When our spouse is suffering, that's the time to control our own emotions and work together to figure out a solution. Whether it be a career crisis or not bringing in enough money, we can help them find ways to make positive changes. Remaining positive is key, not allowing emotions of fear or anxiety cause discord.

Still, though your ability to help is limited, especially if your loved one is continually miserable and complaining day after day without ever taking steps to remedy the situation, be patient. Pray for compassion and try to see the situation in a different light. You are not fighting against your child or spouse but rather, you are warring against strongholds, negative thought patterns, and stress.

For we wrestle not against flesh and blood, but against principalities, against powers, against the rulers of the darkness of this world, against spiritual wickedness in high places. Ephesians 6:12

Find out if the person wants or needs your input. If you're just a sounding board, and it never ends, then you'll have to use one of the methods listed later in this guide to help you find relief. Relationship stress is sometimes at the root of someone's unhappiness. A friend might confide in you about their life behind closed doors. If they're in danger, use your judgment and consider seeking help for them. I know this is touchy.

Once I was extremely stressed because I suspected a friend was being physically abused by her husband. She wouldn't admit to it. She claimed she was clumsy. I felt like she was brainwashed. I felt like he was a coward. I knew I couldn't share my emotions with her. It would only alienate her. I kept my calm and told her I'd always be there whenever she needed me. I did tell her that if I felt her life was ever in danger, I would call the police, with or without her permission. I gave her resources for shelters and encouraged her to get out. None of us are here to be doormats or punching bags.

Abuse is one of those subjects that really pushes my buttons. I hate bullies. I hate people who prey on others. I had to step back emotionally. If I didn't control my own thoughts and actions, I would be no good for her when she needed me. I didn't want him to know how I felt either. I didn't want to chance him influencing her not to speak to me anymore. She needed a positive safe environment and I had to keep my calm so that I could offer that support when she was ready. I also had to pray for wisdom and peace while being there for her.

"I shall stay calm in moments of stress and anxiety, so as to allow positive thoughts and actions to manifest from me." Len Brown

Money stress is common for many people. Some friends or family might just be venting and sharing, whereas others are telling you in an effort to get you to bail them out of a money mess. I've been in both situations and both can be stressful. In the first case, of venting, I listened. But I'm a strong believer that I should help where I can. For instance, one of my aunt's was venting about her bills and how purchasing propane for the winter was going to be a burden. So I offered (insisted) help. Use your best judgment. I also had an acquaintance who constantly got into money binds because of poor spending habits. I'm not judging here. This person would purchase an expensive pair of shoes instead of paying their utility bill and then call around for people to bail them out. I admit I did help the first couple of times.

Health stress is one situation where you can help a friend or loved one shoulder the burden. If a friend needs to talk about their battle with cancer, for instance, then it's helpful if you're there for them, even offering to run errands or go to appointments with them. To help you deal with this stress, you can practice stress-relieving measures yourself. We pray always, but there are other things I do to relax like, hot baths, aromatherapy, or exercising.

With health stress, if it's short term, it probably won't be an issue. But if you know someone dealing with long-term, or terminal illness, be careful to stay calm and not allow yourself to become overwhelmed. Ask God to help you be the calm in the midst of their storm. When my aunt was going through her illness, she had certain people she enjoyed being around because she said we calmed her spirit. It was tough, but God was there every step of the way. That's what we, as believers, should do for each other. We should calm each other's spirits. But we can only do so when our own spirits are calm and Christ-centered.

Being positive in a negative situation is not naïve, its leadership.-Unknown

You have to gauge which type of stress your friend or family member is presenting. Is it something where you should be there for them unconditionally, or is it a situation where you're exposing yourself to someone who refuses to take responsibility and merely wants another person to feel the pain with them? I know it's difficult, but you have to take your emotional health into consideration. You can't help anyone if you're out of control yourself. Remember, just because someone is complaining to you or sharing their problems, it doesn't mean that they necessarily want to take steps to improve their situation.

"Some people don't necessarily mean you any harm but they don't do you any good either...it's called dead weight. Remove it."

Skip the pity parties. It's okay, go ahead and un-invite yourself! Chronic complainers don't really want help or solutions. They really just want you to be there to listen and witness their emotional meltdown. You don't have to, so if you can avoid doing so, by all means, get away.

Health Issues Caused By Stress

I do not fix problems. I fix my thinking. Then problems fix themselves.-Louis Hay

Let's talk about the health issues a bit. I believe our health truly is our wealth. And the enemy knows that so he tries to stress us out to the point of no return. He wants us to be sick and unhealthy. He wants us to die and not witness the Gospel. So let's not be ignorant of his devices. Let's be wise about our health and the effects of stress and the impact of constant emotional turmoil.

Studies show that older adults, women in general, especially working mothers and pregnant women, less-educated people, divorced or widowed people, people experiencing financial strains such as long-term unemployment, people who are the targets of discrimination, uninsured and underinsured people, and people who simply live in cities all seem to be particularly susceptible to health-related stress problems.

Here's an excerpt from an interesting piece I read online:

...individuals can take up to a year to recover a healthy immune system following the death of their spouse, and long-term caregivers have suppressed immune systems compared with persons in the general population. Studies on survivors of sexual abuse and those with post-traumatic stress disorder suggest they have elevated levels of stress hormones, as do students at exam time. In these groups of people and others experiencing loneliness, anger, trauma and relationship problems, infections last longer and wounds take longer to heal.

However, having fun with friends and family seems to have the opposite effect on our immune systems. Social contact and laughter have a measurable effect for several hours. Relaxation through massage or listening to music also reduces stress hormones.

How Does Mood Effect Immunity, by Jane Collingwood **(**http://psychcentral**.com)**

Isn't that something? When our mood is poor, we are not just "in a bad mood". We are in an unhealthy mood. We are negativity impacting our health. And, in essence, we are tearing down our temple (1Cor. 6:19-20)

Ms. Collingwood also says in her article that stress results in increased risk of arthritis and multiple sclerosis. And can worsen skin conditions like psoriasis, eczema, hives, and acne. What's worse, stress can also trigger asthma attacks. I've personally experienced the worsening of acne and asthma attacks brought on by stress.

Additionally, our emotional health influences how we perceive what is happening to us. People who are less emotionally stable or have high anxiety levels tend to experience certain events as more stressful than healthy people do. And the lack of an established network of family and friends predisposes us to stress-related health problems such as heart disease and infections. Caregivers, children, and medical professionals are also frequently found to be at higher risk for stress-related disorders.

Job-related stress is particularly likely to be chronic because it is such a large part of life. Stress reduces a worker's effectiveness by impairing concentration, causing sleeplessness and increasing the risk of illness, back problems, accidents, and lost time. At its worst extremes, stress that places a burden on our hearts and circulation can often be fatal.

A stress-filled life really seems to raise the odds of heart disease and stroke down the road. Researchers have found that after middle-age, those who report chronic stress face a somewhat higher risk of fatal or non-fatal heart disease or stroke over the years. It is now believed that constant stress takes its toll on our arteries, causing chronically high levels of stress hormones and pushing people to maintain unhealthy habits like smoking.

Simply put, too much stress puts you at dire risk for health problems. Whether it comes from one event or the buildup of many small events, stress causes major physical alterations that often lead to health problems. Here is a list of some of these changes:

Stress is always with us controlling what we do and how we feel. If you're stressed, you do things faster and in an unhappier way. Although you don't want to overreact to stress, you don't want to just hide your stress either. Ignoring your stress will only eat at you, hurting your emotions and your relationships. By being aggressive toward another person, you temporarily feel relief, but then reality kicks in as you feel more stressed from hurting the other person.

We need to learn ways to manage our stress and not let it get the better of us and the people we see daily. Stress can motivate us to take action and get our behinds in gear. But, too often, stress works against us. That's why we must manage it effectively. Here are a few Do's and Don'ts:

1) Don't worry – Worrying is extremely dangerous for your health. By worrying, you increase the chances of having a heart-attack and you become miserable.
2) Don't beat yourself up or stress over, "What if…" or "What might happen…" Stop trying to predict the future. You cannot control everything. Ask God for help with what is in your control and give the rest over to Him.
3) Don't involve too many people – If someone isn't involved, just leave them out of the situation. Things will only become worse when they start throwing their emotions into the mix as well. It is so tempting to release your stress on other people. But remember, not everyone can handle your problem. They may become more stressed than you and they may even try to solve the problem or act on your behalf. I've seen this happen when couples fight and involve others. Family and friends become upset and take matters into their own hands, causing the stress to increase for everyone involved. If you must, limit yourself to one or two level-headed people only.

4) Do Take Responsibility – When you take responsibility, you live in truth. You do not become a victim of others. You begin to control and create your feelings. You stop blaming others for what has happened to you and you become proactive controlling thoughts, feelings, and stresses. By accepting responsibility as way of managing stress, you begin self-control.

5) Do Use Self-control – You are in complete control of your emotions. It's by learning to manage your mind that you correctly manage your stress. No matter how badly you want to "go off" on someone, don't. It will only stress you out more in the long run. There is always a chance that you will have to face this person again. You don't want to do anything to hurt someone else. Remember, you have complete control of your emotions and actions. However, your ability to be in control of your emotions and actions is dependent on your desire and discipline to do so.

6) Do Be Self-Aware – You need to manage yourself and control your emotions. You need to be aware if you are treating a person in an appropriate way because of the stress. You need to know that you are stressed, why you are stressed, and ways to manage the stress.

7) Do Push Forward –Winston Churchill said, "If you are going through hell, keep going." Don't stop and give up. I encourage you to stop, relax, and be smart, but do not lose the perseverance to keep going. If you are going through a bad patch in life, by stopping there, you remain in the bad patch. Don't get stuck. Keep it moving.

8) Do Go on a Retreat –If you can afford a holiday, go for it! For those who can't do that, take a stay-cation, stay home turn off phones and social media and just recharge. Take long walks or work out. You may just need to go away for a bit to refresh your mind. By being active, you release hormones that counteract stress.

Stress can make us miserable if it is not managed. Learn these ways to manage your stress, and you'll have stress working for you and not you for it.

Vitamins and Minerals and Stress, Oh My!

Medical research has proved that during stressful situations, particular vitamins are needed to maintain proper functioning nervous and endocrine systems.

Deficiencies of vitamins B-1, B-5, and B-6, can lead to anxiety reactions, depression, insomnia, and cardiovascular weaknesses, while vitamins B-2 and niacin deficiencies have been known to cause stomach irritability and muscular weakness. Their depletion lowers your tolerance to and ability to cope with stressors.

One widely popular theory is that the body's need for vitamin C increases when under stress. Vitamin C is stored in the adrenal gland. After the gland releases adrenal hormones as part of the stress response, the supply needs to be replenished. The production of adrenal hormones is accelerated by vitamin C. Vitamin C is also needed for the synthesis of the thyroid hormone. Thyroid hormone production regulates the body's metabolism. Thus, when the metabolic rate increases under stress, so does the need for vitamin C.

Stress management is a lifelong process. With a successful stress management program, you'll note positive changes in your health, well-being, relationships, and overall performance.

Don't let the enemy use stress to destroy you and the people you love. Control your emotions and manage your stress. Remember: "No temptation has overtaken you except what is common to mankind. And God is faithful; he will not let you be tempted beyond what you can bear. But when you are tempted, he will also provide a way out so that you can endure it." (1Corinthians 10:13). You can do it!

Chapter 3: Deliver Me From Misery Loves Company

We talked about contagious people earlier, but let's talk a bit more about the purposely miserable people. Instead of being inspired by your positive outlook and using it to improve their own lives, *Misery Loves Company* prefers to drag you down with them. You know, "Misery loves company." They want to not feel so alone, and if you allow them to, they'll chain you to their problems, which isn't healthy for either of you.

Luckily, there are a couple of simple things you can do to minimize stress they bring on. There are some people who you have to (or want to) continue being around. For these individuals, we need to have a plan in place where you can manage their stress so that it's not affecting you. This is a situation where you know ahead of time what you're getting into, and yet you're able to prevent their troubles from infecting your own life. There are three ways you can achieve this.

First, try steering conversations away from the repeat stress topics. For example, let's say your coworker is also a good friend but continually gripes about their spouse every time you are around them. I've had this happen to me and it's not fun. It reached the point I was exhausted hearing about it and I began avoiding this person completely. What could have been a great friendship eventually fizzled out because I just couldn't take it. I have a real issue with people who continually complain but never take steps to make changes. The best thing to do is acknowledge what they say, offer condolences that they're going through that, and then perk the conversion up to something more positive. For example:

Friend: "Robert really gets on my nerves. He never spends time with me anymore. All he does is hang out on those stupid social media sites day and night."

You: "I understand that must hurt your feelings. Hey! Why don't we go shopping next weekend? Have you been to the new outlet across town? There are some great deals!"

By acknowledging, you let them know that you were listening. You showed that you cared by offering condolences. But instead of hopping down the emotional bunny trail with them, you offered a positive spin on the situation. If they try to drag you back into the conversation, just nod, and say, "I'm sorry." and change the topic again. I do this all the time. It's better than zoning out on them completely or allowing them to dump their negative emotions on you.

Try not to ask questions or be a relationship counselor, you'll soon find out that you aren't qualified to deal with their issue or they will blow you off completely and continue ranting. This will only frustrate you. If you want, get the business card of a relationship counselor and say something like, "I remembered our talk. I thought about you and picked this up the other day as I'm not equipped to help you deal with it, so I hope this helps!" and then change the subject to a more positive topic.

The second thing you can do is build yourself up in faith. Shield your heart and mind by praying and reading scripture before you see them. Ephesians 6:11 warns us, *"PUT ON THE WHOLE ARMOR of God, that you may be able to stand against the schemes of the devil."* If you're able to do this, your friend can mutter on and on about their woes and you'll be just fine nodding your head, sympathizing, and never let it invade your emotional well-being. While they're going on and on about how miserable they are, you're thinking of the scriptures like Philippians 4:8-9:

"Finally, brethren, whatsoever things are true, whatsoever things are honest, whatsoever things are just, whatsoever things are pure, whatsoever things are lovely, whatsoever things are of good report; if there be any virtue, and if there be any praise, think on these things....and the peace of God shall be with you."

This can take a little practice, but I'm telling you it works. Once you get it down, you will be able to let what they are saying go in one ear and out the other. I know it sounds rude. But, it's not. It's self-preservation, more than anything. You're consciously putting up a barriers so their negative emotions aren't absorbed into your soul.

You know the negativity has penetrated if, after having contact with family either by phone or in person, you become depressed, argumentative, self-critical, perfectionistic, angry, combative, or withdrawn. It's as if you've been contaminated with negativity.

Sometimes, when you're unable to distance yourself in one way (like becoming emotionally un-invested in their issues), you have to distance yourself a different way - physically.

A third option for escaping other people's drama is to walk away. It doesn't mean you have to cut all ties. (Although, in extreme cases, that may be what has to happen, depending on how bad it's affecting you and your family).

"As for a person who stirs up division, after warning him once and then twice, have nothing more to do with him," Titus 3:10

Set a limit on your phone conversations. If your friend has a habit of calling you after work and droning on and on for two hours about their horrible life, make it a point to end the conversation at a certain amount of time, like 15-20 minutes. In fact, you might tell the person when they first call that you can't talk long.

Meet with them in settings where other people or distractions are present. These kinds of stressed people usually want all of the attention on themselves. They don't want to share the spotlight, so by forcing it to be in a place where your attention is divided, they'll feel less like sharing - or if they do, you'll easily be able to get out of the conversation and seek relief.

"I urge you, brothers and sisters, to watch out for those who cause divisions and put obstacles in your way that are contrary to the teaching you have learned. Keep away from them."

Romans 16:17

Be honest with them about how their stress is affecting your life. Some people just aren't aware of how they act. In a loving way, let them know that you care about them and sympathize with their situation - but you have to alleviate stress in your life for your own reasons, so you'll need to keep the conversation light. Now what **true** friend wouldn't understand that?

It's okay to set these boundaries. They are needed if you are going to win the battle of controlling your emotions and not allowing outside influences to take you on an emotional roller coaster ride.

Deliver Me From The Enemy

Let's not forget that we have an adversary, the Devil, the originator of *Misery Loves Company*. He is the most miserable soul of all. He's so miserable that he has made it his mission to make as many of us miserable, angry, depressed, and oppressed as he possible can when we are here on earth. We've talked a lot about the people in our lives and how their negative emotions can influence ours, but we always have to remember that it's possible that they are being negatively influenced by the enemy.

Keep them in prayer. Pray for yourself and your family daily that you do no fall prey to the negative influences of the enemy. The depression, anger, guilt that weighs you down is not from the Father above. If you have any emotions that are uncontrolled, violent, or hurtful, don't just ignore them. Pray for help and guidance. Ask God to help you address them. He loves you dearly and wants you to live a joyful and peaceful life.

For we wrestle not against flesh and blood, but against principalities, against powers, against the rulers of the darkness of this world, against spiritual wickedness in high places. –Ephesians 6:12

Chapter 4: Emotion Control: A Look At Anger

Anger is an emotion that makes your mouth act quicker than your brain. Take a deep breath and think before you speak.

I mentioned anger earlier. And how I use anger emotions to motivate me. Let's talk more. It takes two people to have an argument and it's often the case that each person "fuels" the anger and the emotions in the other by extending and aggravating the tone of the conversation. As the situation continues like this, it is more likely to end up in a confrontation and generate a bad ending.

It's important to exercise emotional control and to be able to control the messages that you send to your brain, to reduce the likelihood of an emotionally charged reaction. Always try and avoid extreme reactions to any situation. Anger is a real problem in today's society. Just watch the evening news and you're bound to see a story about someone losing their cool at work, school, or even the local department store. For this reason, it is important that we learn how to cope with anger issues. As believers, we want to be part of the solution, not the problem.

Everyone, at some time or another in their lives, has experienced anger and perhaps even lashed out in anger. I always marvel at Jesus' display of anger in the temple. The thought of Jesus becoming so upset that he flipped over tables, just astounds me. (Matthew 21:12) *Did He lose control? What was He thinking? Did He feel regret afterward?* I'm going to ask Him when I meet Him. But I digress. So....If Jesus became so angry that he did something like that, what does that mean for little old us? Can we truly control our anger?

"Be ye ANGRY, and SIN NOT: let NOT the sun go down upon your wrath." Ephesians 4:26

Anger is a natural emotion, because we all become hurt, aggravated, insulted, or feel threatened from time to time. Anger can be your greatest ally or your greatest foe. For example, if we feel threatened by another person and we express our anger in a controlled way, the outcome can be favorable. Conversely, if we become out of control, the situation can escalate and become worse than it was before.

NEGATIVE EMOTION + NEGATIVE MEDITATION = NEGATION REACTION
NEGATIVE EMOTON +POSITIVE MEDITATION=HEALTHY EMOTIONAL RESPONSE

When we control our thoughts that lead to our emotions, we benefit tremendously. Our emotions become healthy responses. They protect us and warn us of imminent danger. They tell us when something needs to change. And they help us handle crisis situations. However, if we allow our anger to get the better of us, we put our well-being, our health, and, sometimes, even others at risk.

But the fruit of the Spirit is love, joy, peace, patience, kindness, goodness, faithfulness, gentleness, self-control; against such things there is no law. Galatians 5:22-23

I remember feeling terrified as I witnessed a family member allow her anger to get the best of her. Someone was threatening her child and she reacted in such a way that I'd never seen. It was as if she wasn't herself anymore. She was yelling and cursing. Then, she abruptly hung up, dashed to her gun case and took out a pistol. Shocked and scared, I tried to talk her out of leaving. But she sped off in her car determined to "set them straight". Thankfully, no one was hurt. By the time she reached her destination, she'd decided to leave the gun in the car. The situation did become pretty heated, but there was no violence or use of weapons.

It is not uncommon for someone to ignore the problem in dealing with anger. The person might be in denial of any negative behavior he or she has exhibited. Denial is a big reason why some people never deal with their problems, or their anger.

"Anger is a sign that something needs to change." Mark Epstein

I know that a person can only take so much before they blow their top at some point. And we all have a boiling point. Some of us have higher capacity to handle stressful triggers than others. Part of the problem is, somewhere down the line, we weren't given the tools to deal with our emotions effectively. I know, growing up, it wasn't something that we discussed. In my family, we simply suppressed our emotions. As a result, there are some of us now, as adults, who have serious anger issues (don't tell them I said that-smile).

Uncontrolled emotions are complicated and damaging. They can sap the life from a person. Therefore, when we know how to cope with our feelings and emotions, we are on a path to success. Nothing is more gratifying than feeling a sense of control. It's a personal achievement that is vital to our emotional well-being and our spiritual walk.

Surrounding yourself with positive people is so crucial. When we surround ourselves with positive people, we will pick up their positive habits. But if we are spending time with hot-heads, chances are, we will be influenced by their negative attitude. And when trouble comes, we are more likely to lose control.

Have you ever had an emotional outburst? Do you remember how you felt immediately following? You probably remember feeling disappointment, frustration, embarrassment, and maybe even sadness. Losing control is not very pleasant and, deep down within ourselves, we know that it's simply "not right." The feeling you get in the moment immediately following the outburst is your indication. I have read about people who have no remorse, conscience, or moral compass, but those people have a personality disorder. If you don't have a personality disorder or illness and your anger is out of control, simply put, you need help.

As peacekeepers, we have a responsibility to practice anger control. If you're having trouble in this area, here are a few tried and true ways to diffuse and or manage your anger: **Counting To 10 Actually Does Help.** You have probably heard people advise you that you should count from 1 to 10 whenever you begin to feel angry. As crazy as this sounds and as difficult as it might be to do whenever those emotional feelings are welling up inside you, it's amazing what can happen if you physically do employ this tactic. It absolutely can help to diffuse your temper.

Stop Engaging And Walk Away. In our crazy, stereotyped society, it might be seen as weak to actually turn and walk away from an emotive situation. Doing so, however, will almost invariably diffuse the situation and the person who initiates this movement is ultimately the stronger of the two. This is one of the best ways of controlling anger, but it's not to say that you should let those emotions bottle up inside you, either. You do need to address the situation that's causing the disagreement or confrontation, but must do it in a controlled and non-confrontational way. If you let it stew up inside, that's not healthy either.

Often, anger management control is rooted in an ability to be rational and to be able to identify solutions to any problem or situation. If you can come up with a solution that will include, if necessary, the ability to "own" the problem, then you will already be looking at this from a positive angle.

Consider Other Perspectives. Sometimes, your anger may well be justified but you have to deal with it in a calm way. When you can feel the emotion of anger beginning to bubble over, you have to be able to look at the situation from every possible anger, not just your own point of view. Any attempt at a confrontational approach will likely initiate angry defensive mechanisms in everyone involved.

Do Something Constructive. When I begin to feel myself becoming angry, I do something productive. My favorite thing to do is cleaning. The chores need to be done anyway and by the time I'm done, I've calmed down, the cleaning is done, and I feel better. Another thing I do is workout. I plop in a workout dvd or lace up my sneakers and head to the park or local track.

Stop And Smell The Blessings. Okay, the saying is "smell the roses" but in this case, try counting your blessings. Think of the good things that are happening in your life. Think of something that you have to be grateful for. Remember "…think on these things and the peace of God will be with you." (Philippians 4:8)

Anxiety Attacks

You will keep him in perfect peace, whose mind is stayed on you, because he trusts in you. (Isaiah 26:3)

The first time I had an anxiety attack, I had no idea what was happening. I was driving home, thinking about my marriage and contemplating divorce. My then husband and I had gotten into a terrible argument and we'd decided to separate. I remember, out of nowhere, I began feeling like I couldn't breathe. I was taking deep breaths but it wasn't working. I let the windows down and inhaled the evening air. It seemed to help. And remember thinking, "This is stress and I have to let it go." The rest of the drive home, I tried to focus on other things, my son, my nieces and nephews, anything that made me happy. By the time I made it home, I was breathing normally. That experience taught me that stress can, and will, trigger anxiety.

Anyone who has ever suffered the horror of a panic attack knows that they are real, even if they are very difficult to quantify or describe. Sometimes, these attacks can last for minutes on end, which, in turn, feel more like hours. It's important to be able to get to the bottom of any triggers and to try and make changes to your life accordingly.

If you want to know how to stop anxiety, then you have to understand why you are anxious. You might think that the answer to that question is rather easy to come up with, as the majority of us face so much on any given day that an elevated level of anxiety is simply understandable.

You may have money issues, job worries, health concerns, or all three at the same time. If you have a lot of time on your hands, then you may have a tendency to sit and reflect too much on the wrong things, all of which can help to contribute to the feeling of anxiety.

If you find that an attack seems to come out of the blue, ask yourself exactly what you were doing immediately before. There are almost always triggers, but they may not be as obvious. Remember that certain stimulants, such as those that are found in coffee, energy drinks, and cigarettes can be to blame. If you haven't been eating properly or sleeping as well as you should, you might be creating a bad environment in this way.

These episodes can be really disturbing and frightening. I know mine was. When you feel one coming on, you want to know how to stop anxiety attack repercussions before they get out of hand. However, sometimes, it can feel that merely focusing on the fact that you might be having an attack can make it worse. Some people suggest breathing into a paper bag. I'm not sure if this really works. I know that it at least makes you to slow down and focus on your breathing. (Inhaling slowly through the nose, before exhaling steadily and slowly through the mouth). This can, in turn, help to slow down your heart rate and fend off the attack itself.

If life seems overwhelming, try to remember this prayer: "God, GRANT ME THE SERENITY to accept the things I cannot change; courage to change the things I can; and wisdom to know the difference." Take one day at a time. By focusing only on one issue before you move on to the next, you can start to make sense of it all. When your racing thoughts just accumulate everything together until it becomes one big problem, it can all seem to be insurmountable. The problem begins to magnify.

Don't be afraid to evaluate your thoughts and emotions to find the potential causes of the attacks. In other words, don't just bury your pain. Deal with it. But deal with it knowing that you have the power of God backing you. By figuring out what's causing the attacks, you won't invariably bring on one of the attacks, but you will be able to identify some of the steps you can take to help avoid them in the future. Take one step at a time, dealing with and hopefully eliminating the potential triggers. If money problems are a trigger, find out what God says about your finances. *2 Corinthians 9:8 says: "And God is able to make all grace abound toward you; that ye, always having all sufficiency in all things, may abound to every good work." Whenever we need money or possessions, prayer is the answer. Look to the Lord, because He will provide it-according to His will.*

Meditate on His word and clear your mind of doubt. Praise God for His goodness. Put on some worship Music and worship your provider. Offer a sacrifice of praise (Hebrews 13:15). I know from experience that anxiety will flee when you emerge yourself in praise and worship. The Lord inhabits the praises of His people (Psalm 22:3). And when God comes in Anxiety runs out kicking and screaming!

Depressed Thoughts

God said don't look around because you'll be impressed. Don't look down you'll be depressed; just look to me and you'll be blessed.-unknown

When my 46 year old mother died suddenly of a pulmonary embolism, I went into a depression. I didn't want to get out of bed. I didn't want to pray. I didn't want to do anything but lay in bed and cry. I felt like I was surrounded by an invisible barrier. I was in a bubble. And the last thing I wanted to do was "talk about it". Depression can manifest itself in many different ways. You might have a feeling of hopelessness, which can lead to withdrawal, inactivity, and a complete lack of productivity.

You might feel as if you're not able to concentrate at all and just can't get down to work as you used to. You might also feel as if you're tired, have no motivation or energy whatsoever, yet have considerable difficulty sleeping. Do you lie awake in bed for hours on end, only to find that when you do get to sleep you have difficulty waking up and listening to that alarm bell?

Depression is a very serious matter, which does not discriminate. Depression does not care what your age is, what gender you are, or even what your race or social class is. Depression can often make a person feel sad, helpless, hopeless, and irritable. It is normal for people to have these feeling sometimes, but some people cannot just snap out of it and this is the difference between what is normal and major depression. It is the determination and brutality of the emotions that determine the mental illness of depression from normal mood changes.

A Prayer Against Depression

God, I have been carrying a heavy burden and I am coming to You right now for relief. I surrender all my hurts, disappointments, and insecurities to You. Thank You for Your Word, which tells me about Your unconditional love and affection for me. You are my Father, and I am Your child. I love to be in Your presence, You are the source of all my peace and joy. Forever I will praise You. Amen.- Joyce Meyer

Depression is an illness that affects your body, mind, disposition, thought, sleep, energy, concentration, weight, and much more. Depression is not a mood, and it is not a sign of personal weakness. Clinical depression is constant and can interfere significantly with an individual's ability to function by emotional experiences of sadness, loss, or passing mood states. If you are depressed, don't ignore it, but don't give in to it either. Clinical depression can be devastating to all areas of a person's everyday life, including family relationships, friendships, and the ability to work or go to school.

I want to mention another type of illness that involves depression. That is Bipolar disorder (manic-depression), a mood disorder or abnormalities of mood. Bipolar disorder involves episodes of both serious mania and depression. Bipolar disorder, like clinical depression, can have a devastating impact on sufferer's life if it is not treated. I've witnessed untreated Bipolar disorder and it's very frightening, especially if it's someone you care for deeply. Acknowledging that there is a problem and getting help is so important.

Major depression is a more common illness, the symptoms of which are mainly those of 'low' mood. Someone close to me had major depression and it lead to his complete breakdown. He finally accepted that he needed help and he saw a doctor. Today, he is living much healthier and happier and his family reunited and happy.

If you're feel low constantly, you don't want to get out bed, easily frustrated, and feeling sick all the time, you may be experiencing depression. The immune system of a depressed person is usually very low and, therefore, ineffectively responding to diseases, including cancer. It's important that you deal with it immediately, not just for you but for the people you love. They are suffering, too. When you are feeling depressed, you tend to push other people away from you and it's unfortunate that many people are not able to recognize the symptoms of depression in others, or to be sympathetic. As we are all supposed to be "tough" in this society, people have a tendency to tell you to "snap out of it", or something similarly unhelpful.

"Mental pain is less dramatic than physical pain, but it is more common and also more hard to bear. The frequent attempt to conceal mental pain increases the burden: it is easier to say "My tooth is aching" than to say "My heart is broken."
— C.S. Lewis, *The Problem of Pain*

If you have been feeling depressed for a long period of time, but are unable to explain why or know what to do about it, you need to take action. Sometimes, you need significant lifestyle changes. If you have a tendency to drink too much or use other drugs, this is almost certainly contributory. If you have a lot of time on your hands then you can often let your racing, and maybe negative, thoughts take over. Lifestyle changes can help to make a difference.

We are not what happens to us, who we get to be is who we say we're going to be in the world-Gary of ProjectForgive.com

All of us will feel depressed at one moment or another but for many, like myself, thankfully, these feelings dissipate and go away. However, in quite a significant number of people, depression can be difficult to deal with and even life altering. And triggers such as relationship ending, a death in the family, or loss of a job can have a devastating impact. If you're feeling depressed or down, there are some simple steps you can take on your own to start improving your mood:

**Start your day with an inspirational quote or scripture reading.

**Have a good look at what you eat. Are you getting the right amount of vitamins, nutrients and minerals? Many advocate a diet that is rich in vegetables and fruit and has a good amount of omega-3 fatty acids.

**Get out and about as much as you can and soak in some of the warm sunlight, within reason, of course.

**Take up a new hobby or pastime and is definitely the time to seek out people who are invariably happy, positive, and upbeat.

**Dedicate time to prayer and meditation. Use a simple inspirational devotional or read passages from your Bible. Never be afraid to reach out to wise counsel, specialist, or medical professionals if you think that you cannot cope any longer with this depression. Recognize self-destructive behavior, especially over reliance on alcohol as a prime example and seek help, if necessary, to control this, too.

Depression is definitely treatable, whether through prescription drugs, alternative medicine, counseling, lifestyle changes, or a combination of all of these. You don't have to suffer through it, needlessly. For GOD HAS NOT GIVEN US a spirit of fear, but of power and of love and of a sound mind. (2 Timothy 1:7)

Peace.
It does not mean to be in a place where there is no noise,
trouble, or hard work, it means to be in the midst of those
things and still be calm in your heart.-unknown

Chapter 5: Finding True Happiness

"I let go. I accept my life as it is. I do not judge. I do not dramatize. I let life's events come freely and I welcome the lessons they convey. I stop struggling now. I let go and know that God always gives me that which is most appropriate for my soul."

Almost everyone have heard the hit single, *Don't Worry, Be Happy* by Bobby McFerrin. The song has a very catchy way of conveying its message of being happy to everyone. Bobby McFerrin's simple message surely made a lot of people by telling them not to worry.

"Come to me, all you who are weary and burdened, and I will give you rest. Take my yoke upon you and learn from me, for I am gentle and humble in heart, and you will find rest for your souls. For my yoke is easy and my burden is light." (Matthew 11: 28-30)

We've already covered the health risks of stress. So by now, you know that stress brought on by constant worrying is linked to top causes of death such as heart disease, cancer, and stroke. These reasons alone should encourage us to live a stress-free life.

There may be a tiny percentage of people who want to be miserable. But for the most part, I believe we all want to live a happy, resilient, and optimistic life. Being happy is "characterized by characterized by or indicative of pleasure, contentment, or joy."

I believe the key words in that definition are contentment and joy. There are two scriptures dealing with these subjects that I live by and I think they will be a blessing to you as well.

"Not that I speak in respect of want: for I have learned, in WHATSOEVER STATE I AM, therewith to be CONTENT." (Philippians 4:11)

**"Consider it pure joy, my brothers and sisters, whenever you face trials of many kinds, because you know that the testing of your faith produces perseverance." – James 1:2-3 (NIV).

Being happy is not about your circumstances being absolutely perfect. It's about finding inner peace and joy in life, despite the trials and challenges. But how do you do that? You make up your mind that you are going to trust beyond yourself. That anything out of your control is still in God's control. Knowing that what you are experiencing will work to your advantage, somehow. And more importantly, you don't have to know how. It may hurt temporarily but it will not hurt forever. One day, you will wake up and everything will be okay.

Abraham Lincoln observed that most people, most of the time, can choose how happy or stressed, how relaxed or troubled, how bright or dull their outlook to be. "Folks are usually about as happy as they make their minds up to be." You see, in his mind, the choice is simple really, choose to be happy. Not because of an outside influence, but an internal choice.

Here are some ways to keep negative emotions at bay and achieve internal happiness:

**Be grateful. We have so much to be thankful for. Thank the waiter for bringing your food, the housekeeper for keeping your home, the babysitter for watching your kids. Also thank the carrier for delivering your packages, thank the policeman for making your place safe, and thank God for being alive.

**Watch the news less. It's stressful. Some people just can't start their day without their daily dose of news. Think about it, 99% of the news we hear or read is bad news. Starting the day with bad news does not seem to be a sensible thing to do.

**A spiritual connection is vital. Being part of a good church, Bible study, or other God-centered group with its singing, sacraments, prayers, and meditations can help foster inner peace.

**Manage your time. Time is invaluable and too important to waste. Time management can be viewed as a list of rules that involves scheduling, setting goals, planning, creating lists of things to do, and prioritizing.

**My favorite thing to do- Laugh! Laugh and Laugh heartily every day. Heard a good joke? Tell your friends or family about it. As they also say, *Laughter is the best medicine.* Psalm 126:2 says, "Then was our mouth filled with laughter, and our tongue with singing: then said they among the heathen, The LORD hath done great things for them."

**Try not to keep anger or frustration pent up, this is bad for your health. Instead, find ways of expressing them in a way that will not cause more injury or hurt to anyone. Express your feelings, affections, friendship, and passion to positive people around you. They will most likely reciprocate with words of encouragement and comfort that will inspire you.

**Finish a project. Hard work and completing a task brings tremendous personal satisfaction. It gives a feeling of being competent and capable. During one my most difficult times, I redecorated my dining room. It turned out beautiful and really lifted my mood. As I sit in it typing today, it still makes me happy. Accomplishments are necessary for all of us, they give us a sense of value. Work on things that you feel worthy of your time.

**Another one of my favorites- Learn something new. Try and learn something new every day. Learning also makes us expand and broaden our horizons. And could also give us more opportunities in the future.

**I know I've said this in other chapters, but exercise is so good for your emotional health. Run, jog, walk, and do other things that your body was made for. Feel alive.
**Avoid exposure to negative elements like loud noises, toxins, and hazardous places.
And always remember the quote from Abraham Lincoln, he says that, "Most people are about as happy as they make up their minds to be."

Learning To Love Yourself

The second greatest commandment: YOU SHALL LOVE YOUR NEIGHBOR AS YOURSELF. (Mark 12:31.)

Love yourself. Accept yourself. Embrace your personality and yes, even your imperfect emotions. Know that Jesus died for you because He knew you had flaws. And He still wanted you to be reconciled with the Father so that you would have eternal life. You don't have to be perfect or get it all right today. As long as your heart is right before God and you are making progress, that's what counts.

How can we fulfill the command to love our neighbors, if we cannot love ourselves? We need to be filled with the unconditional love of a healing God, before we can forgive others or be healed of emotional challenges ourselves. Be thankful and appreciate how God made you.

Understand that if there is a problem with your emotions, your health, or your physical body, your Creator is ready and willing to help you. He loves you tremendously. Rejecting or hating yourself is not what God wants for you. Self-hatred is no more from God than uncontrolled emotions are. God is a God of love and order. "For GOD is not the author of confusion, but of peace," (1Corinthians 14:33)

"Whoever does not love does not know God, because GOD IS LOVE." (1 JOHN 4:8)

THANK GOD FOR CREATING YOU IN HIS IMAGE. ACCEPT THAT HE SAYS YOU ARE "FEARFULLY AND WONDERFULLY MADE". YOU MAY NOT FEEL LIKE IT TODAY. AND YOU CERTAINLY MAY NOT FEEL LIKE IT WHEN YOUR EMOTIONS GET THE BEST OF YOU. YOU ARE MORE THAN A MERE PHYSICAL BODY. YOU ARE MORE THAN YOUR EMOTIONS. INSIDE YOU DWELLS A PERFECT SPIRIT.

Psalms 139:14, "I will praise thee; for I am fearfully and wonderfully made: marvelous are thy works; and that my soul knoweth right well."

Get rid of the notion that you have to be perfect. Only God is perfect (Mark 10:18). His son, Jesus was crucified for your imperfections. Stop trying to crucify yourself. Christ paid it all. God loves you. And He wants you to see yourself the way that He sees you. As a marvelous creation. I know you want a better life and you deserve one. You deserve peace. You can be free from destructive emotions and misery-loving people. The next time you feel like your emotions are trying to take control, stop yourself. If necessary walk away. Listen to the still small voice in your heart saying, "Peace be still". That voice is the Creator, the one who loves you beyond measure. Know that you are fearfully and wonderfully made. You don't have to act out to prove a point. Christ proved your point on the cross. Live the abundant life He died for you to experience. A life of order, peace, prosperity, and love. God bless.

Find Your Peace
"Ego says: Once everything falls into place, I'll find peace.
Spirit says: find your peace, and then everything will fall
into place." –Marianne Williamson

Chapter 6: Quotes About Emotions

Never reply when you are angry. Never make a promise when you are happy. Never make a decision when you are sad.
Some days you can't make heads or tails of life. These are the days to put stress aside and do what feels good to you. Tomorrow is a new day and things will make sense given time.-Anna Pereira
One who has control over their emotions has great power over those who don't!

Acting is not being emotional, but being able to express emotion.-Kate Reid

Love is not an emotion. It is your very existence.

Rather than being your thoughts and emotions, be the awareness behind them.

Your emotions are the slaves to your thoughts, and you are the slave to your emotions.

I keep my emotions buried under the floor. Locked up deep, where they can't hurt me anymore.

No emotion is the final one. - Jeanette Winterson

Reason generates the list of possibilities. Emotion chooses from that list. –Dale Peterson

Emotion is energy in motion. - Peter McWilliams

When you welcome your emotions as teachers, every emotion brings good news, even the ones that are painful.

Human behavior flows from three main sources: desire, emotion, and knowledge. –Plato

I haven't got that kind of discipline where I can turn my emotion inside out and then just switch off. It affects me fairly profoundly and I don't like putting myself through that kind of mincer every day. -Jimmy Nail

Negative emotions like hatred destroy our peace of mind. -Matthew Ricard

Wit is the epitaph of an emotion. –Friedrich Nietzsche

Unexpressed emotions will never die. They are buried alive and will come forth later in uglier ways. –Sigmund Freud

An emotion can best be viewed as an energy that comes to you for healing.

And if thought and emotion can persist in this way so long after the brain that sent them forth has crumpled into dust, how vitally important it must be to control their very birth in the heart, and guard them with the keenest possible restraint.-Algernon Blackwood

Emotion is the poetry of life.

Don't stress. Look up to God. Hand it back to him and He will turn it all around.

Thank you for reading this book. If you enjoyed it I hope you will take a moment to leave a review on Amazon.com. God bless you.

BONUS BOOK

51 Ways to Love Your Enemies

How To Love Others When They Are Hurting You
Lynn R Davis
Copyright © 2013
Get FREE BOOK notifications. Click to enter your email
address: http://www.Lynnrdavis.com

51 Ways Excerpts

"They hate you and maybe you hate them too. You're sick and tired of being mistreated and you've had enough. You're at your wits end. *Who do they think they are anyway?* The last thing you want to do is "lose your religion", tell them where to go and how to get there..."

"I'm writing *51 Ways to Love Your Enemies* because I'm going through something painful right this moment. I feel betrayed. My natural instinct is to retaliate and strike back. But God has a better plan. He tells us to love our enemies and do good to those who hurt us. It's so hard, but I know He would not ask me to love them unless I was able to-with His help."

Introduction

Love your enemies because they are the instruments to your destiny. - Joseph Campbell

Love + Enemies = Reward

They hate you and maybe you hate them too. You're sick and tired of being mistreated and you've had enough. You're at your wits end. *Who do they think they are anyway?* The last thing you want to do is "lose your religion", tell them where to go and how to get there. On top of that, God says, "love your enemies?" But somebody needs to set them straight. And why can't it be you? You're more than ready to handle the task.

I feel your pain. Somebody does need to do something. That somebody is you. And that something is **love them**. We cannot draw others to the Kingdom if we are acting just as evil and unloving as they are. God is not pleased when we bicker and fight. We don't glorify Him and it's counterproductive to our mission. Jesus knew that we would have enemies. He had plenty. Jesus' enemies were some of the most mean-spirited, backbiting, two-faced folks you'd never want to meet. But He loved them just the same. And He commanded us to love our enemies as well. We don't have to like their lying, manipulation, gossiping, or selfishness. Matthew 5 doesn't say, "Hang out with your enemies on weekends and invite them to your family reunions". Jesus' instruction was to, "love them; do good toward them; and pray for them." We are commanded to *Agape* love them, not like them.

God's Kind Of Love

Agape love is unconditional, self-sacrificing love. God loves us unconditionally, no matter what we do. And He wants us to love others the same. So don't expect hugs and kisses from your enemy for your acts of kindness. Instead, look to God. Please Him and expect great favor, blessings, and love to flow into your life from the Father.

It doesn't sound logical to the natural mind. But we are spiritual creatures and our methods for obtaining victory must be spiritual as well. God is love. You have the nature of God in you. You are stronger than you think. You can love your enemy. It won't be a cakewalk, but your victory over anger, hatred, and strife will be sweet.

It hurts to be hurt. But It Feels Good To Love

I'm writing *51 Ways to Love Your Enemies* because I'm going through something painful right this moment. I feel betrayed. My natural instinct is to retaliate and strike back. But God has a better plan. He tells us to love our enemies and do good to those who hurt us. It's so hard, but I know He would not ask me to love them unless I was able to-with His help.

I'm sharing my experiences in hopes that you, too, will find the courage to overcome evil by doing good. I believe the items listed demonstrate the love of God. Any way you choose to love your enemy is a blessing not only to them but to you as well. Our Father is wonderful. He blesses us when we are a blessing. We have that assurance and we rejoice.

You can refer back to this scripture reading from time to time while reading the list:

"(43) Ye have heard that it hath been said, Thou shalt love thy neighbor, and hate thine enemy. (44) But I say unto you, Love your enemies, bless them that curse you, do good to them that hate you, and pray for them which despitefully use you, and persecute you; (45) That ye may be the children of your Father which is in heaven: for He maketh his sun to rise on the evil and on the good, and sendeth rain on the just and on the unjust. (46) For if ye love them which love you, what reward have ye? Do not even the publicans the same? (47) And if ye salute your brethren only, what do ye more than others? Do not even the publicans so? (48) Be ye therefore perfect, even as your Father which is in heaven is perfect." Matthew 5:43-48

Not all of the items listed are discussed in great detail. I think of this book is a work in progress because God is working with me in this area even as I write. That said, you will notice that I do go into quite a bit of detail on some listed items. That's because I felt some of them are so important that they deserved a devotional of sorts. If you just choose one or two of those ways to show love toward your "enemy," I'm sure the rest of the ways will fall into place.

In this book "enemy" refers to anyone who has wronged or committed some hurtful or damaging offence to you. Some of the ways listed are really simple whiles others are more challenging. Always be prayerful in what you do. Do not try to force others into acceptance. Allow the love of God to draw them. Christ said, "If I be lifted up I will draw all men unto myself." Demonstrate the love of Christ in your daily interactions with people and He will do the rest. If you remember nothing else remember, **Love + Enemies = Reward**.

1.   Don't Condemn Them

Judge not, and ye shall not be judged: condemn not, and ye shall not be condemned: forgive, and ye shall be forgiven - Luke 6:37

It's easy to give yourself over to a condemning spirit. Especially when you have been hurt deeply or been mistreated in a way that you feel should be vindicated. We pass blame and condemn the other person—while ignoring the possibility that we may have played some role ourselves. We have to remember that we are not all knowing. Only God truly knows the reason an enemy behaves the way they do.

One of the definitions listed at dictionary.com for the word condemn is: to express an unfavorable or adverse judgment on; indicate strong disapproval of; censure.

In Romans 8:1 we are assured as Christians that we are not condemned for our sins because Christ has set us free from judgment and of sin and death. Christ loves us and therefore He does not condemn us. As Christians we strive to be like Christ. One way for us to be like Him is to not condemn those who wrong us. No matter how unfair or vile their actions may be. We just don't have the right to pass judgment.

The benefit in not condemning is found in Luke 6:37, "that ye shall not be condemned." This is a great blessing, certainly because we ourselves have done wrong things that could easily be held against us, but also because we are shown grace and found blameless in Christ Jesus. Why? Because of love. We have received Christ's gift of freedom from condemnation. Out of love we should extend that same liberating gift to our enemies. And in return we will receive compassion and generosity from God and others.

Pray for help in this area: "Father thank you for not condemning me and loving me unconditionally even when I don't deserve it. Help me, Lord, to be more like you in this area so that I do not condemn my enemy, but I show them how the love of Christ sets us free from sin."
Compassion will cure more sins than condemnation - Henry Ward Beecher

2-11 Practical Ways to Love Your Enemies

Invite Them To A Ministry Event. Everyone likes to be invited. Whether or not they attend is up to them. It doesn't have to be a ministry event, it could be some other social event or luncheon, etc. that you think they might enjoy. Choose an uplifting event like a concert, don't invite them to a seminar for difficult people.

Buy Them Tickets To A Local Venue. Often there are local venues that host musical events or festivals for a small cost. If you think they would be interested, by all means buy some tickets and offer them. If they don't accept the tickets you can use them yourself or give them away.

Pick Up The Tab. If you happen to be in line ahead of them tell the cashier you want to buy their soft drink, coffee, or meal. This is an easy way to show kindness and of being thoughtful that can really make a loving impact on the receiver.

Compliment Them. You'd be surprised the positive impact a compliment has. It doesn't have to be over the top. A simple, "That color looks good on you," often works wonders.

Acknowledge An Accomplishment. It's always nice to be recognized for an achievement. So go ahead and congratulate them or tell them what a nice job they did. Don't be concerned that they never acknowledge your accomplishments. It's not about being nice to people who are nice to you. It's about loving your enemy.

Celebrate Them. Everyone has a birthday. Send an email birthday card or create a small banner for their office or work space. If nothing else, just say, "Happy Birthday!" Maybe you heard that their anniversary is coming up? Buy a card or coffee mug with a nice message on it.

Support Them. Find out about a cause or charity that interests them and be supportive whether it's going through your closet to donate to a shelter, volunteering your time, or contributing to a special foundation.

Make A Sacrifice. Give up your place in line. Or offer those free movie tickets that you won in a raffle. Sacrifice something that you enjoy by offering it to them.

Teach Them Something That You Know. We all have unique knowledge, skills, and abilities. If you know how to do something that could be helpful to them, why not offer to teach them?

Learn From Them. If there is something that they do well that you admire, tell them you admire it. "I really like the way you..." and then let them know that you'd enjoy learning from them sometime.

12.   Show Compassion

But whoso hath this world's good, and seeth his bother have need, and shutteth up his bowels of compassion from him, how dwelleth the love of God in him? - 1 John 3:17
The love of God is very powerful and if that powerful love resides in us, how can we not have mercy and compassion for the hurting? Remember your enemy is hurting. Hebrews 5:2 says, "who can have compassion on the ignorant…for that he himself also is compassed with infirmity." Whether you see your enemy as hurting or as ignorant, God still wants you to love them by being loving and sympathetic.

It doesn't sound logical, I know, to feel sympathy for someone who is hurting you, but you must remember that they are worse off than you realize. I mentioned once before in my bestseller, *Deliver Me from Negative Self-talk*, that hurting people hurt people. Your enemy is hurting. You can't see why. And you don't have to. God didn't tell us to figure out why, He just said love them.

Another component of compassion is the desire to alleviate suffering. When it comes to our enemies, the last thing we feel like doing is alleviating anything. Your enemy is suffering in his own private hell. They are angry, unhappy, and don't see a way out. Your compassion is their way out. Your Christ-like behavior shows them that no matter what life throws at you, you can still have peace and compassion in your heart.

Some people think only intellect counts: Knowing how to solve problems, knowing how to get by, knowing how to identify an advantage and seize it. But the functions of intellect are insufficient without courage, love, friendship, compassion and empathy. - Dean Koontz

13-22 Practical Ways to Love Your Enemies

Encourage Them. If you see them having a bad day, say something encouraging or uplifting.

Share A Motivational Resource. Perhaps you receive daily motivations, quotes, or stories. Share a little motivation with them. Maybe they too could use a little boost.

Put Yourself In Their Shoes. Show empathy for a situation or circumstance they may be dealing with.

Control Your Tongue. No matter how badly you want to say something negative in response to their actions, don't. Resist gossip. It only causes more ill will and hurt feelings. Try not to talk about them with anyone else unless it's to say something positive. Remember there is a chance that what you say may be twisted and turned by the time it gets back to them. And make no mistake, it will get back to them.

Stand Up For Them When They're Right. If you notice that they are being unfairly treated, stand up for them to defend them. It may catch them off-guard but it shows that you are a person who believes in what's right no matter what.

Don't Retaliate. If they do something to hurt you, do not seek revenge or do anything to "get them back." The Lord says vengeance is His.

Speak Blessings Over Them And Their Family.

Intercede For Them. If you know they are going through a tough time or that they are in need of something, intercede on their behalf.

Avoid Conflicts. There may be areas in which the two of you strongly disagree. Do not rub your differences in their face. Don't bring up how much you dislike something that they love just to get a rise out of them. Avoid causing conflict.

Keep The Peace. This is similar to avoiding conflict. If other people are involved and causing drama, do not participate. Maintain a position of neutrality and a peaceful disposition.

23.   Be Civil

If thine enemy be hungry, give him bread to eat; and if he be thirsty, give him water to drink: (22) for thou shalt heap coals of fire upon his head, and the Lord shall reward thee. - Proverbs 25:21-22

Another way to love your enemy is to be civil, or in other words, be polite and courteous. It's never beneficial to be rude. Even when your enemy is being rude to you.

This act of love is one that I had a personal experience with.

A particular young lady in a church I attended seemed to always treat me with disdain. Whenever I was nearby, she'd make it a point to look at me, roll her eyes, and then smile at some other person nearby. It was almost as if she wanted me to feel snubbed. The first time it happened, I was really hurt. I'd never done anything to this person, so I didn't understand. So the next time I saw her, I greeted her. She didn't respond, but simply acted as if she didn't hear me. Part of me wanted to ask, "What's your problem?" But I knew the type of person she was, that saying this would only aggravate the situation. So I let it be.

For the remainder of my time at that church, I chose to be civil toward her. Whenever I saw her I smiled and greeted her without worrying about whether or not she would reciprocate. You see, I realized that God's command to love is not predicated on the other person's attitude toward me.

I wish that I could tell you that her heart changed and we became friends, but that's not the case. She remained cold and indifferent. However, God did bless me with a peaceful spirit. My attitude toward her changed. I didn't see her as a bad person. I saw her as a hurting person. And the love of God in me manifested courtesy and politeness.

Some people will not change immediately. Some may never change. But what is important is that we represent Christ. Be civil. Be polite and kind. You will grow spiritually in ways that will lead you to future victories in life.

Be civil to all, sociable to many, familiar with few, friend to one, enemy to none. - Benjamin Franklin

24-33 More Practical Ways to Love Your Enemies

Make A Gesture of Kindness toward something or someone they care about. Buy a stuffed toy for their pet or a cool action figure for their kid.

Be Patient With Them. Remember that none of us are perfect and Christ is patient and loving toward us and we should also be patient with others. Love is patient.

Be Kind To Them. Resist the temptation to treat them the way that they treat you.

Be Humble. Have a spirit of humility in their presence. You don't have to be timid, but don't try to be intimidating. Love is humble.

Be Polite. Polite people are easier to be around. Rude people encourage more rudeness. Create an environment of peace by being polite. Love is polite.

Don't Allow Yourself To Be Provoked. Be strong. Don't allow your emotions to be controlled by someone else's actions. Just as Christ was not provoked by Satan, do not allow yourself to be provoked by their actions. The enemy knows how to push your buttons. Don't allow it! Take a deep breath. Count to ten. Stand in love. Love cannot be provoked.

Be Truthful About The Situation. If the relationship is strained because of something you've done, be truthful. Apologize. If not, pray about it. But be truthful with yourself and them about what is happening. God is love. Love is truthful. The truth sets us free.

Do Not Envy Them. It may seem that they have the upper hand, but they do not. It rains on the just and the unjust. God will not be mocked and His word will not return void. If He said you will be rewarded, you will be. Love is not envious.

Stand Strong In Faith. One of you needs to be in faith in order for deliverance to take place. Stay in faith so that the eyes of their understanding will be opened.

Stop Keeping Record. Love does not keep record of wrong. By doing so you give the enemy the opportunity to bring up time and again the pain and hurt that you've endured at the hand of the enemy. Plead the blood of Jesus over the painful memories and make the decision to stop recording the wrongs and recalling them over and over again day after day, month after month, year after year. Let it go.

34.   Be Grateful For Them

*"For in the time of trouble He shall hide me in His
pavilion: in the secret of His tabernacle shall He hide me;
He shall set me up upon a rock. And now shall my head be
lifted up above my enemies round about me: therefore will
I offer in His tabernacle sacrifices of joy; I will sing, yea, I
will sing praises to Yahweh." -Psalms 27:5-6*

What? I know, you're thinking I'm nuts right about now
for telling you to be grateful for the coworker who just
tried to get you fired, the family member that stabbed you
in the back, or the nosey neighbor who reported your less
than immaculate lawn to the Homeowner's Association—
been there done all of that!

The truth in the Word though, is that God will make all of
these challenges work together for our good. Because we
love God, our desire is to please Him. And it pleases Him
when we do good to evildoers. And He in turn rewards us.
So try seeing your enemy as one of the avenues by which
you will be blessed. They are another opportunity for you
to receive a blessing from God. And we know that God is
not stingy with blessings. So when we love our enemies
through gratitude, we not only experience a sense of
victory, we also enjoy the benefits of fulfilling the will of
God that qualifies us for His reward (Proverbs 25:21-22).
Be grateful that your enemy has offered you yet another
opportunity to be blessed and receive favor from God. The
more enemies you have to love, the more rewards you have
coming your way!

*Our enemies provide us with precious opportunity to
practice patience and love. We should have gratitude
toward them.* - Tenzin Gyatso, The 14th Dalai Lama

35.   Smile At Them

A smile makes people happy. Good news makes them feel better. - Proverbs 15:30 (Easy-to-Read Version)
I don't mean break out a huge "God's-gonna-getcha" grin on your face every time they walk by. But rather a gentle smile that says, "Christ loves you and so do I," or at least, "Christ loves you and I'm trying my best." But by all means please resist the urge to scowl whenever you're in the presence of a perceived enemy.

Not many people can refuse a smile. There have been times in my life when the mention of certain names could cause my eyes to roll and my nostrils to flare. It's been said that smiles are contagious. Who knows? Maybe your smile will make your enemy feel better. Though it may make them happy only for a moment, your reward from the Father will be eternal. And you will be happy for an eternity.

It takes a spiritually mature person to smile at someone who has caused them pain. How mature are you? Test yourself. The next time you see your enemy flash those pearly whites, just think of the reward that's coming your way. Show your enemy the love of Christ in your return smile.

It is almost impossible to smile on the outside without feeling better on the inside. - Unknown

36-45 Practical Ways to Love Your Enemy

Love Yourself. You cannot love others until you love and accept yourself. Hurting people hurt people. Loving people love people.

Seek Godly Council. Talk to a person of authority who is spiritually mature. Avoid people who have negative advice and try to convince you to seek revenge. Instead, select someone who will be objective enough to correct you if you need to be corrected and provide Godly wisdom about the circumstances.

Don't Faint. "Be not weary in well-doing for in due season you will reap if you faint not." Hold on. (Galatians 6:9)

Stay In The Word Of God. "Faith cometh by hearing and hearing by the word of God." It takes faith to deal with hurt and people who cause pain. You are better able to love them, when you are walking by faith, staying in the word, and seeking God daily.

Shine Before Them. Let your light shine. (Matthew 5:16) Be joyful in the Lord no matter what. Though you shed a tear over the situation, you are not without hope. The Lord is your strength and redeemer. Remember the Joy of the Lord is your strength. (Nehemiah 8)

Transform. Refuse to handle the situation from a fleshly perspective. The flesh is enemy to God. Be transformed in your thinking. Study the word. Renew your mind about the enemy. Walk in victory over the adversary. (Romans 12:2)

Resist Fear. "God has not given you a spirit of fear but of sound mind, power, and love." When you walk in the power of God, you will increase in confidence and *demonstrate* the power and love of God. (2 Timothy 1:7)

Know The Real Enemy. "We wrestle not against flesh and blood, but against principalities, against powers, against the rulers of the darkness of this world..." When you know that the real enemy is not your neighbor, you are better able to see them as a brother or sister created by God and therefore worthy of love.

Pray For Unity And Oneness. Pray that you continually walk in unity so that your enemies will see your heart and believe that Christ is Lord. (John 17:20)

Handle Issues In A Godly Manner. "If thy brother shall trespass against thee, go and tell him his fault between thee and him alone: if he shall hear thee, thou hast gained thy brother." (Refer to Matthew 18:15)

46.   Forgive Them

So shall ye say unto Joseph, Forgive, I pray thee now, the trespass of thy brethren, and their sin; for they did unto thee evil: and now, we pray thee, forgive the trespass of the servants of the God they father. And Joseph wept when they spake unto them. - Genesis 50:17

I love the story of Joseph. It just blows my mind how he was able to forgive his brothers after they sold him into slavery and caused him so much pain. Joseph was able to look past what they'd done to see how God was able to make something good come from his years of suffering at the hands of others.

Though your enemies have evil intentions, God is able to make your enemies become stepping stones to your success. Author Joseph Campbell said, "Love thine enemies because they are the instruments to your destiny." You can only be successful in forgiveness when you take your eyes off the gravity of the offense and trust God. Joseph's brothers didn't deserve forgiveness and perhaps your enemy doesn't deserve your forgiveness either. But just as God forgives us when we don't deserve it, we should forgive others.

However wicked the betrayal may be, stop giving in to feelings of resentment toward them and pardon the offense. Stop playing reruns of the day you were betrayed. Your mind is far too precious to allow the sewage of un-forgiveness to stagnate and eventually stink up your life. Forgiveness is a pathway to spiritual growth as well as physical and emotional well-being.

To forgive does not necessarily mean you have to forget. I know some people say otherwise, but in my opinion, how else would you learn from your mistake and avoid repeating it? Just because you forgive someone doesn't mean that you have to trust them. Trust is earned. Forgiveness is a gift of love. Give your enemy the gift of forgiveness and trust God to work all things together for your good.

Always forgive your enemies—nothing annoys them so much. - Oscar Wilde

47.   Lend Them A Hand

If thou see the ass of him that hateth thee lying under his burden, and wouldest forbear to help him, thou shalt surely help with him. - Exodus 23:5

Showing your enemy love by lending a helping hand wasn't first introduced in the New Testament as many think. God introduced the concept of helping our enemy as a law from the beginning in Exodus 23. God made it a law that required that a person who saw his enemy's animal fallen down because of a heavy load, should stop and offer a helping hand. Can you imagine seeing your enemy stranded on the side of a highway with a flat tire? What would you do? Would you stop and offer help or drive past without a second thought?

I personally know several people who would say, "Oh well, that's their problem." But that is not the way to show the perfect love of God. If we are people after God's own heart, our first desire should be to please Him with our actions. It pleases God when we represent Him in a way that draws others to the kingdom.

Find a way to lend your enemy a hand. It doesn't have to be anything complicated. It could be something as simple as opening the door for them when their hands are full. You could help them with a project that they are having trouble completing. Keep your eyes open for small but loving ways to lend a helping hand.

It's important for us to not only sing about helping others but actually doing something about it. - Mark Lee

48.   Be Prayerful

But I tell you who hear Me; Love your enemies, do good to those who hate you, bless those who curse you, pray for those who mistreat you. - Luke 6:27-28

Don't use your words to curse your enemies. Instead, go to God in prayer petitioning for deliverance. Go to God for guidance about what should be done. Trust God and pray that His justice prevails.

Prayer is such a powerful way to express love for your enemy. As Jesus suffered on the cross he prayed, "Father forgive them for they know not what they do." (Luke 23:34). What an amazing and powerful display of love for Him to pray for people who had just physically assaulted him and spit in his face!

Hebrews 12:2 tells us that Jesus endured the shame of the cross because of the joy that awaited Him. No matter what your enemy has done, always remember that loving them ultimately brings you a joyous reward from the Father.

Sample Prayer: Father I thank you for being a God of justice and peace. Lord I have been wronged and I don't know how to handle the situation. Please guide me and help me to walk in forgiveness toward them. Heal the resentment and anger in my heart. In Jesus Name. Amen

Remember, resist the natural urge to gossip and speak negative words of anger about your enemy. Instead choose to speak to God in prayer.

A wise man gets more use from his enemies than a fool from his friends. - Baltasar Gracian

49.   Be Understanding

He who gets wisdom loves his own soul; He who keeps understanding will find good. - *Proverbs 19:8*

If I had to admit one thing about my enemies, it's that I really can't say that I know them very well. Aside from the rare occasion of falling out with a family member, the "enemies" I've encountered have been people on various jobs or acquaintances from various social groups.

Because I don't know them very well, I'd be lying if I said I understood them. I don't know why they behave the way they do. I don't know what they've been through or where they come from that effects their thought process. In grad school I took a creative thinking class. One of the topics was assumptions—why we make them and how they affect our decisions and actions.

Every decision we make or action we take is based on an assumption. And that assumption is based on factors like our upbringing, cultural beliefs, past experiences, etc. The dangerous thing about assumptions is that our minds take for granted that they are true— regardless of what anyone else thinks. And we begin to think that our point of view is the absolute end all, be all. We then use these beliefs to draw conclusions about people and circumstances. And our actions, good or bad, are a direct result of what we assume to be true—whether that truth is right or wrong.

When two people have two entirely different upbringings or past experiences, they may also have opposing assumptions which in turn causes conflict and disagreement. Problems arise when neither party is willing to challenge their own assumptions or understand the other person's perspective. As Henry Winkler put it, "Assumptions are the termites of relationships."

I believe praying for wisdom and understanding is key to loving your enemy. Ask God to give you a heart of understanding so that you are not blinded by your own assumptions. Seek to understand where your enemy is coming from. There's a good chance that something you don't understand about them is fueling the tension between the two of you.

The creative individual has the capacity to free himself from the web of social pressures in which the rest of us are caught. He is capable of questioning the assumptions that the rest of us accept. - John W Gardner

50.   Search For The Good

Therefore if there is any consolation in Christ, if any comfort of love, if any fellowship of the Spirit, if any affection and mercy... - Philippians 2:1
As the saying goes, "If you look for the bad in people expecting to find it, you surely will." Is it hard to look for the good in the bad? Yes. But there is always a great reward. It's worth the effort.
If you have the spiritual maturity and the emotional fortitude, you can search for the good in your enemy. Seek the good and you will find the good. While on earth, Christ experienced hurt and pain from those who made themselves His enemies. But He still chose to love them. The entire time He walked with Judas, He knew that Judas would betray Him. But there is never any indication in scripture that He treated Judas badly. When we seek to have the attitude of Christ toward others we demonstrate Jesus' example of compassion for others. It's a choice to seek the good in others. A choice that is challenging and unpopular. But we aren't called to be popular. We are called to effect change.

Our behavior towards others should bring out the best in others. Matthew 5:13 asks the question, "but if the salt loses its flavor, how shall it be seasoned?" We are the salt of the earth, intended to improve the tastes of life. Our attitudes should never leave a bad taste in anyone's mouth no matter how much they hurt us. David demonstrates how to love our enemy by seeking the good in 2 Samuel 1:17-27. Even though Saul made David's life miserable and even tried to kill him, David chose not to speak evil of Saul. Instead, David used his musical talent to write and perform a beautiful song for Saul's funeral. David chose to see the good in Saul. He choose to see Saul through the eyes of God. We are all His children, created by Him. And if God created your enemy, surely there is something good in them. It may be buried under years of hurt and pain, but it's there waiting to be awakened or at least nudged by your Christ-like attitude toward them.

The good neighbor looks beyond the external accidents and discerns those inner qualities that make all men human and, therefore, brothers. - Unknown

51.   Be Respectful

Look, this day your eyes have seen that the Lord delivered you today into my hand in the cave, and someone urged me to kill you. But my eye spared you, and I said, 'I will not stretch out my hand against my lord, for he is the Lord's anointed.' -1 Samuel 24:10

Very often we run across people in positions of authority whose personalities clash with our own. So much so that we may consider them an adversary. I mentioned David and Saul in the previous chapter and I will use them here again. David had opportunity to kill Saul for everything that he had done to him, including seeking to kill him. But David chose to recognize that Saul was God's anointed and not harm him. David respected Saul as a chosen man of God.

When we cross paths with people in positions of authority whose ideas and values clash with our own, it can be difficult to see them as anything other than the enemy. When this happens feelings get hurt resulting in bad blood between the authority figure and subordinate. This is just a bad situation all the way around. The person in authority can really make the work environment difficult.

I've even come across authority figures who purposely pit themselves against their subordinates out of arrogance when they should see them as team members and treat them respectfully. No one wins. Leaders should never be rude, condescending, and abusive. If you are in a situation where the "enemy" is a person of authority, I urge you to do what David did. Try to view them as God's creation whom He loves. Pray for strength and compassion.

Remember your promotion comes from God, not your boss. The person in authority may have control over certain aspects of your position, but God has the ultimate authority- over them and your situation as a whole. The control they think they have is fleeting because it is not rooting in love. Respect their position and pray for them. Then, because of your obedience, expect your promotion, breakthrough, or blessing to come from God.

When you make your peace with authority, you become authority. - Jim Morrison

Conclusion

I'm not going to try to polish it up and make it look pretty. It's ugly. It's painful. It's tough. Loving your enemies is not for the faint of heart. It's hard work. And it takes courage. But it's worth the work. If you can master loving your enemies, your spiritual maturity will soar to new levels. If you are facing an enemy or adversarial situation, I encourage you to please consider using the principles in the Word. Consider loving your enemies.

Remember Proverbs 25:22 says we heap coals of hot fire on our enemy's head when we are kind toward them. If it helps, think of it that way. You're pouring hot coals on their head by being nice to them!

Anytime I am offended, I start implementing some of these items immediately. I take back my power. I know that I cannot allow the anger and resentment that I feel to rule over me. Doing so would open the door for the enemy to bring more strife and pain; ruin my ability to effectively represent Christ, and eat away at me emotionally. I don't want that to happen to me or you. There's no reason for either of us to be defeated. Not when our Father has given us a formula for success.

Love + Enemies = Reward.

I'm already starting to feel better, stronger, and more like the conqueror I was created to be. We can do this. We will win.

These things I have spoken unto you, that in me ye might have peace. In the world ye shall have tribulation: but be of good cheer. I have overcome the world. - John 16:3

Made in the USA
Columbia, SC
31 July 2018